To Fran Penner

ISBN 0-439-49145-2

Text copyright © 1995 by Lucille Recht Penner. Illustrations copyright © 1995 by Jada Rowland. All rights reserved. Published by Scholastic Inc., 557 Broadway, New York, NY 10012, by arrangement with Random House Children's Books, a division of Random House, Inc. SCHOLASTIC and associated logos are trademarks and/or registered trademarks of Scholastic Inc.

12 11 10 9 8 7 6 5 4 3 2 1   3 4 5 6 7 8/0

Printed in the U.S.A.   23
First Scholastic printing, September 2003

The Statue of Liberty

by Lucille Recht Penner

illustrated by Jada Rowland

SCHOLASTIC INC.

New York Toronto London Auckland Sydney
Mexico City New Delhi Hong Kong Buenos Aires

A lady stands in
New York Harbor.
She is as tall as a
skyscraper.
She is called
the Statue of Liberty.

"Liberty" means freedom.
All over the world,
people dreamed
of coming to America
to find freedom.

People came by ship.

The trip took many days.

Men, women, and children
were crowded together.

They were tired, hungry,
and scared.

Suddenly they saw the lady!
They had reached
America at last.
Now they knew
they were free.
People cried for joy.

The Statue of Liberty

was a present

from the people of France

to the people of the

United States.

A Frenchman made the lady.

His name was

Frédéric Bartholdi.

He copied his mother's face

for his statue.

How beautiful she was!

First Frédéric made
a small statue.

Then a bigger one.

Then an even
bigger one.

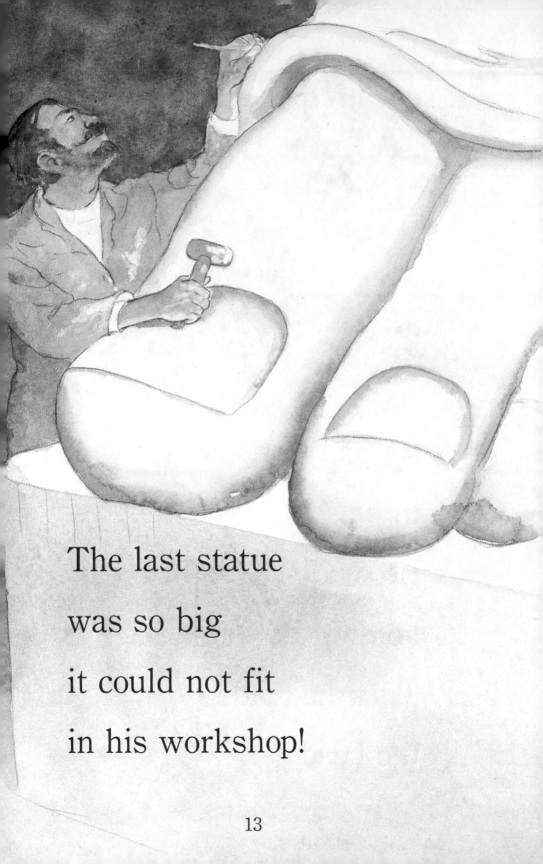

The last statue
was so big
it could not fit
in his workshop!

He had to make it
in pieces.

He made the right hand
holding the torch.

Then he made
the head.

Each finger was longer
than a man.
Each eye was as big
as a child.

Frédéric needed
lots of help.
His helpers worked
in a big room.

They took
the pieces outside
and put them together.
She was higher than
all the buildings.
Much higher!

Workers took
the statue apart.
They packed it
in 214 crates.

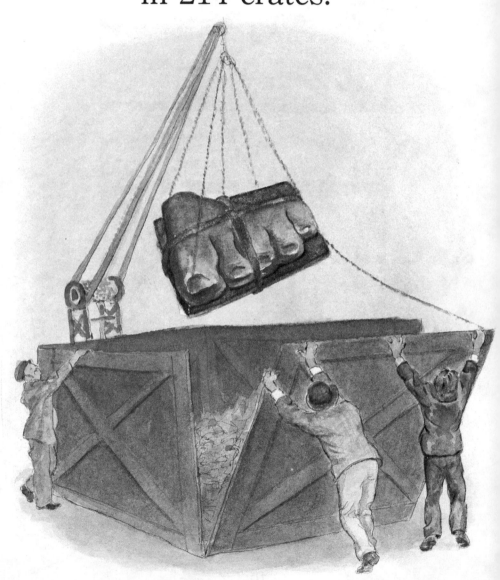

A ship carried it

from France to New York.

In America
the people
were building
a high pedestal
for the lady to stand on.

But they ran
out of money!
The work stopped.
No one knew
what to do.

Joseph Pulitzer owned

a newspaper.

He had an idea.

Joseph said, "The statue
needs a home!
I will print the name
of everyone who gives
money to help."
Thousands of people
sent nickels and dimes.
Children sent pennies.
Soon there was
enough money.

Now workers could finish
the huge pedestal.
They set the lady
on top of it.

26

A big French flag

was draped over her face.

On October 28, 1886,
the people of New York
had a parade
to welcome her.

The President of
the United States
made a speech.
Frédéric Bartholdi
was excited!
He raced up a staircase
inside the statue.
Up and up he went
to the very top.

Frédéric looked down.

A boy was waving

a white handkerchief.

It was the signal.

Frédéric pulled a rope

and the flag fell.

There was the lady!

Hip, hip, hurrah!

Cannons boomed.

Boat whistles blew.

People cheered.

The excitement
never ended.
Today, more than
one hundred years later,
the Statue of Liberty
still welcomes people
to America—
the land of the free.